HISTORY AND GEOGRAPHY 906
THE EARTH AND MAN

CONTENTS

Author: **Don R. Ramsey**
Editor-in-Chief: Richard W. Wheeler, M.A.Ed.
Editor: Richard R. Andersen, M.A.
Consulting Editor: Howard Stitt, Th.M., Ed.D.
Revision Editor: Alan Christopherson, M.S.

Alpha Omega Publications

Published by Alpha Omega Publications, Inc.
300 North McKemy Avenue, Chandler, Arizona 85226-2618

THE EARTH AND MAN

The earth has suffered many terrible shocks throughout the thousands of years man has occupied it as his home. Great changes have taken place in man's environment since earth's divine creation. Many men of science have used the theory of evolution to explain earth's beginning and its history. However, this theory does not include the fact that an almighty and benevolent God created the universe. Evolutionary theory also does not agree with the Biblical account of the universal Flood. Evolutionists believe that life appeared upon the earth through spontaneous, natural processes and changed into its many present forms through billions of years.

Many civilizations have developed since Adam occupied the fruitful garden in Eden. Only by God's grace has man survived centuries of hunger, war, natural disaster, and turmoil. However, man has not only survived, he has learned that the earth is full of resources that can be developed to give him many comforts. A person's responsibility in developing these resources includes caring about and providing for his neighbors and descendants.

The planet Earth does have a future. Many people wonder that if man survives the challenges of controlling land, air, and water pollution, will he then destroy himself in a nuclear holocaust? The Bible is the most dependable source of information concerning the future events that God has scheduled on earth. Wonderful things and some very terrible events will soon affect the whole world. Everyone, especially Christians, should be alert to God's timetable concerning man's future on earth.

OBJECTIVES

Read these objectives. The objectives tell you what you will be able to do when you have successfully completed this LIFEPAC.

When you have finished this LIFEPAC, you should be able to:

1. Tell what clues prehistoric fossils give concerning the earth's origin and the Flood.
2. List three effects of the Flood upon nature and man.
3. Explain how man settled in groups after the Flood.
4. Describe when and how civilizations developed in different areas of the world.
5. Tell the contribution of navigation to the development of nations.
6. Tell the importance of the Industrial Revolution in shaping city life.
7. Outline urban problems as they developed in connection with labor and energy needs.
8. Identify how the environment is affected as man uses the natural resources.
9. Describe the events that will prepare the world for an evil world ruler.
10. Explain what will happen to earth and man's civilizations when Christ comes to judge the world.
11. Describe how God is preparing man for his external habitat.

_____

_____

_____

_____

_____

_____

_____

_____

_____

_____

I. THE EARTH IS MAN'S HOME

A person can attain ownership of something in several different ways. He can purchase it, or he can inherit it. Man can even steal an item or borrow it and not return it. Man can discover property, as Columbus did, and lay claim to it, if no one currently owns it. Man can wage war and claim the spoils of a defeated enemy. Inventors and composers develop and compose new materials; they receive a patent or copyright on their creation and claim the new idea as their own.

God claims the earth as His own because He made it. Genesis 1:1 states, "In the beginning God created the heaven and the earth." King David wrote (Psalm 24:1), "The earth is the Lord's, and the fulness thereof; the world, and they that dwell therein." Man also belongs to God because man was created by Him. Man was created by God to inhabit the earth, and he has been appointed earth's manager and administrator.

In this section you will learn about the earth as man's home. You will learn that man has been given dominion over the earth. Although man has not always exercised his dominion in a proper way, God has not taken away man's dominion. Instead, God has judged man's sin and irresponsibility. You will learn that man was preserved through the judgment of the Flood and was scattered to cover the earth. Finally, you will learn how man's history began.

SECTION OBJECTIVES

Read these objectives to learn what you should be able to do when you have completed this section.

1. Tell what clues prehistoric fossils give concerning the earth's origin and the Flood.
2. List three effects of the Flood upon nature and man.
3. Explain how man settled in groups after the Flood.

VOCABULARY

Study these words to enhance your learning success in this section.

antediluvian (an tē du lü' vē un). Times, people, or events that were before the Flood.

cuneiform (kyü nē' u fôrm). A form of writing using wedge-shaped characters.

deluge (del' yüj). A great flood.

Fertile Crescent (fer' tul kres' unt). An arc-shaped area in the Middle East that lays between the Tigris and Euphrates rivers and was rich in agriculture in early times.

fissure (fish' ur). A crack or opening that runs across the surface of the earth.

fossil (fos' ul). The remains or imprint of plants, animals, and man that are preserved in the rocks of the earth.

hieroglyphic (hī ur u glif' ik). A system of writing developed by the ancient Egyptians using pictures and symbols.

inundate (in' un dāt). To submerge or cover with flood waters.

linguistic (ling gwis' tik). Pertaining to different languages.

petrify (pet' ru fī). The process that turns soft material into a stony substance.

radiation (rā dē ā' shun). To send forth as rays, as of light or heat.

silt (silt) Fine particles of soil and rock carried by water and deposited in a low place.

strata (strā' tu). Natural or deposited layers of material, one upon the other.

tundra (tun' dru). Treeless plains found in arctic lands.

Note: All vocabulary words in this LIFEPAC appear in **boldface** print the first time they are used. If you are unsure of the meaning when you are reading, study the definitions given.

Pronunciation Key: hat, āge, cãre, fär; let, ēqual, tėrm; it, īce; hot, ōpen, ôrder; oil; out; cup, pút, rüle; child; long; thin; /TH/ for then; /zh/ for measure; /u/ represents /a/ in about, /e/ in taken, /i/ in pencil, /o/ in lemon, and /u/ in circus.

MAN INHABITS THE EARTH

Moses wrote (Genesis 2:7-8), "And the Lord God formed man of the dust of the ground, and breathed into his nostrils the breath of life; and man became a living soul. And the Lord God planted a garden eastward in Eden; and there he put the man whom he had formed." The first man was given a beautiful garden filled with every kind of fruit-bearing tree for him to use and maintain. After God created the woman, a helper suitable for the man. He blessed them and gave them the responsibilities of populating the earth and subduing it.

Man was created with high intelligence; he used language and wisdom in carrying out his responsibilities in the garden. An indication of man's intelligence is his assignment of names to every creature God had made. Man also talked with and responded to his Creator in the garden environment.

Although man was a rational, intelligent being, he chose a course of action that would bring death. He disobeyed God. Because of man's disobedience, the ground was cursed and he was removed from the fruitful garden. Obtaining food was now a difficult task for man. The cursed ground yielded many thorns and thistles, and man had to work very hard to obtain enough edible plants for his "daily bread."

Many Christian geologists agree that the environment in which early man lived was spring-like, a "hothouse" environment. A canopy of water vapor shielded earth's inhabitants from the harsh effects of the sun's **radiation** and gave the earth its hothouse environment. The **antediluvian** soil was so rich that it could support large populations of human and animal life. They believe no deserts, polar regions, or towering mountain ranges existed, the land everywhere was much the same. At that time the land was probably just one large continent that would later separate into several continents and drift apart. Dinosaurs and other reptile families wandered over much of the land. These creatures fed on lush tropical greenery that has now completely disappeared. Vast forests that once sheltered many such prehistoric creatures in what is now northern Arizona are now empty sites littered with shattered **petrified** logs. Enormous herds of mammoths roamed what is now the frozen **tundra** of Siberia. Rhinoceroses and walruses shared a swampland in an area of the present-day United States.

A greater variety of plants existed before the Flood than grow in today's world. Trees such as the sequoias of California flourished alongside date palms, breadfruit trees, and banana plants in what is now Alaska. Western Canada produced oak and beech trees with branches that bore the additional weight of hanging grapevines. This solid mass of vegetation was supported by a delightful semitropical climate that did not vary from hot to cold weather extremes.

Complete these statements.

1.1   At Creation, the land consisted of ~~lush vegetation~~ *One large Continent* .

1.2   Petrified logs can be found in northern _Arizona_ .

Write the letter for the correct choice.

1.3   The earth before the Flood had no __C.__ .
  a. mammoths   c. polar regions
  b. lush vegetation   d. animals

1.4   The climate in the beginning of Creation was __b.__ .
  a. harsh   c. frigid
  b. spring-like   d. rainy

1.5   In the beginning a canopy of water vapor shielded man from __C.__ .
  a. frostbite   c. the sun's radiation
  b. the ice age   d. rain

1.6   Dinosaurs were members of the __b.__ family.
  a. primate   c. ark's
  b. reptile   d. mammal

1.7   Because man sinned, the ground was __a.__ .
  a. cursed   c. fruitful
  b. barren   d. hilly

1.8   Breadfruit and banana trees were found in __d.__ .
  a. Alabama   c. Maine
  b. California   d. Alaska

1.9   Oak and beech trees were found in __c.__ .
  a. Northern Mexico   c. Western Canada
  b. Eastern United States   d. Antarctica

MAN SURVIVES THE FLOOD

Genesis 6:5, 7, and 8 states, "And God saw that the wickedness of man was great in the earth, and that every imagination of the thoughts of his heart was only evil continually. . . And the Lord said, I will destroy man whom I have created from the face of the earth; both man, and beast, and the creeping thing, and fowls of the air; for it repenteth me that I have made them. But Noah found grace in the eyes of the Lord."

Noah was a seventh-generation descendant of Adam. Noah was a godly man whom the Lord told to build a large ark. This ark would preserve Noah's family and some of every specie of animal from the universal Flood that was to come. Then, according to Genesis 7:11, ". . . in the six hundredth year of Noah's life, in the second month, the seventeenth day of the month, the same day were all the fountains of the great deep broken up, and the windows of heaven were opened." The great **deluge** resulted in part from the torrential rains that fell forty days and nights.

Some Christian geologists hypothesize that the earth underwent great changes during the Flood. Earthquakes shook the ocean and heaved sections of sea-bottom upward. Tidal waves hit the world's beaches and carried numbers of sea creatures miles inland. Vast chasms opened as underground rivers poured their torrents upward to spread across the face of the earth. Hills toppled into gorges. New steep mountain ranges were pushed high into the surging waters. Hundreds of active volcanoes exploded, only to be buried in the watery depths. New **fissures** were opened through which fresh volcanoes would later be born. Enormous waves rolled trees, herbs, and grass into tangled masses; dropped them into crevices; and smothered them by tons of mud and rock. These deposits of pressed vegetation would eventually be mined as bituminous and other varieties of coal. Boiling minerals and rocky soils were mixed with the bones of many dying things and formed new **strata** in the earth. Oil, called petroleum, also formed from the organic remains. This together with coal, comprises what geologists call "**fossil** fuel."

Meanwhile, Noah and his family busily cared for the needs of their living cargo. For five months the ark floated over the **silted** remains of ancient cities. Finally, it landed on the mountains of Ararat in what is now Turkey. He stayed seven more months in the ark before moving out to establish a settlement in God's clean, reborn earth.

Write the letter if the correct choice.

1.10   Noah was a seventh-generation of _C_.
    a. Enoch   c. Adam
    b. Methuselah   d. Seth

1.11   Rains during the deluge fell for _d_ days and nights.
    a. 120   c. 150
    b. 100   d. 40

1.12   The original earth was greatly changed by _b_.
    a. the ice age   c. a volcano
    b. a deluge   d. an earthquake

1.13   Noah's ark landed on the mountains of Ararat located in _C_.
    a. Russia   c. Turkey
    b. Greece   d. Syria

1.14   In addition to rain, water in the Flood came from __a__ .
         a. underground rivers   c. canyons
         b. volcanoes   d. faucets
1.15   One kind of fossil fuel is __a__ .
         a. petroleum   c. limestone
         b. uranium   d. wood
1.16   The different layers of the earth are called __b__ .
         a. fissures   c. the core
         b. strata   d. fossils

MAN COVERS THE EARTH

In the beginning God had instructed man (Genesis 1:28) to ". . .be fruitful, and multiply, and replenish the earth, and subdue it. . ." Man obviously obeyed the Lord as the original earth well populated by the time of Noah. Before the Flood, man had learned to build cities, enjoy music, and work with metals (Genesis 4:16-24). Man had even devised a code of law and justice.

Following the Flood, man began to rebuild civilization. Communication was no problem to the descendants of Noah. All the people spoke a common language. Noah's sons had learned expert engineering skills from their father. Thus, their descendants, the world's new leaders, made grandiose plans for reconstructing civilization's first city. The people said (Genesis 11:4) ". . .let us build us a city and a tower, whose top may reach unto heaven; and let us make us a name, lest we be scattered abroad upon the face of the whole earth." The city the people began to build was named Babel. Antediluvians had populated the area hundreds of years earlier, but their great cities had been **inundated** by the Flood. Babel was located in the old Mesopotamia valley, between the Tigris and Euphrates rivers. This area is part of a section of land now called the **Fertile Crescent**.

God knew that their plan to build such a one-world city was a challenge to His authority. The Lord had given clear instructions for man to repopulate the whole earth. Because of the people's disobedience, the Lord confounded their common language. As variations appeared in their speech, the people became distrustful of one another because of **linguistic** misunderstandings. Most of the leaders took their families and clans and left Babel to find new places to live. Those who stayed behind in the valley (the Sumerians) developed Babel into a beautiful place called Babylon. The Sumerians also founded other great cities, such as Ur, in the Fertile Crescent.

After man failed in his rebellious attempt to build the city and tower of Babel, he was scattered abroad ". . .upon the face of all the earth." (Genesis 11:9). Descendants of Japheth, one of Noah's sons, moved north with their families and began populating Europe. Tribes that had descended from Ham migrated south and began establishing colonies in Africa. Heading east were descendants of Shem, some of whom soon began farming the fertile Hwang Ho valley of China. By 1400 B.C. these industrious Chinese had developed an organized government and a written language. The Chinese had also founded a religious system that included ancestor worship. Some Asiatic hunters moved farther east and found a land or sea passageway onto the American continent. Soon the entire earth was being explored and settled as man migrated out from Babel.

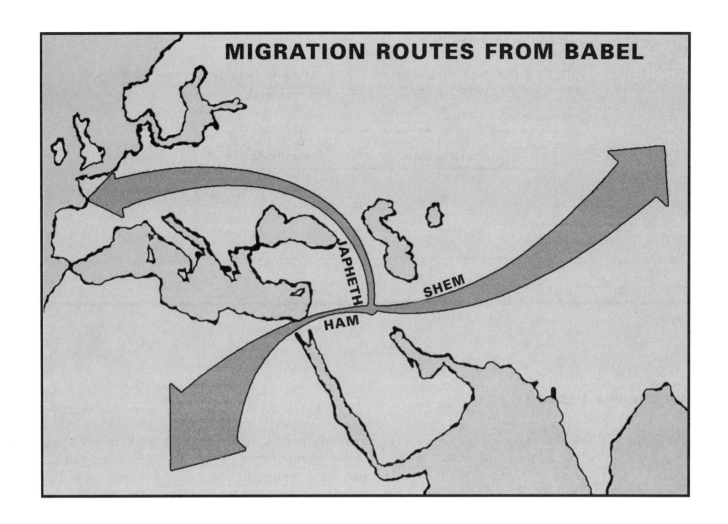

MIGRATION ROUTES FROM BABEL

JAPHETH

HAM

SHEM

►►► **Complete these statements.**

1.17   The area that lay between the Tigris and Euphrates rivers in Mesopotamia is
        called the *Fertile Crescent* .

1.18   The descendants of Noah started to build a city and a tower called
        Babel .

1.19   When the people started to build the city, they all had the same
        language .

1.20   The people scattered to other parts of the world because the Lord
        confounded their language.

1.21   The people who remained at Babel were the *Sumerians* .

1.22   Babel was called *Babylon* by the Sumerians.

1.23   Besides Babylon the Sumerians built the city of *Ur* .

1.24   The Chinese had developed an organized government and written language by
        1400 B.C.

7

Complete this activity.

1.25 Complete the following chart with the names of Noah's three sons and the regions of the world where their descendants migrated.

	Noah's Son	Descendants
a.	Japheth descendants	Europe
b.	Ham	Africa
c.	Shem	Hwang Ho valley China

MAN BEGINS HISTORY

The Sumerians established several city-states along the Tigris and Euphrates rivers. Besides Ur and Babylon they built Kish, Nippur, and other loosely governed communities. Each independent city-state adopted its own religion and built magnificent temples to honor various idol gods. Large libraries in Ur, containing thousands of clay tablets written in wedge-shaped characters called **cuneiform**, have been found by archaeologists. These first books told stories of great leaders and of military campaigns. These first librarians also preserved records of Sumerian laws and religious music. Because these cities were located at the "crossroads of the Middle East," invading tribes eventually began conquering Mesopotamian territories. Under the leadership of Hammurabi, Babylon became militarily ambitious. Its rulers controlled the nearby city-states for almost 200 years. Then, the Hittites and other tribes began their conquest of the Fertile Crescent.

Egypt, another river-valley civilization, was being recognized by other nations as a powerful kingdom under the rule of the Pharaohs. The lower and upper sections of Egypt that lay along the Nile River had been united under Menes (mee' neez) who established Memphis, Egypt's first capital city. The Egyptians learned that papyrus reeds, growing profusely along the banks of the Nile, could be made into paper. This discovery led to the establishment of libraries and schools where information was recorded in **hieroglyphic** writing.

Communication between Middle Eastern nations was strengthened as Phoenician merchants plied their trade throughout the Mediterranean area. These sailors developed an alphabet that would later be adopted by many advancing civilizations. Man was becoming increasingly interested in what was happening in countries and civilizations around him.

One family of historical importance moved during this time from Ur to the land of Canaan. (Canaan lay along the eastern shore of the Mediterranean Sea and was inhabited by Amorite tribes.) Abraham and his family made their new home in the hill country of Canaan. Because he believed God, Abraham received a divine promise that his descendants would have this territory as their homeland forever. During a period of famine, he moved to Egypt but later returned to Canaan. Abraham is recognized as the father of both the Hebrew and the old Arabic nations because these nations are derived from the descendants of his first two sons.

8

Write *true* **or** *false.*

1.26 _true_ The Sumerians established several city-states along the Tigris and Euphrates rivers.

1.27 _true_ Each independent Sumerian city had its own religion.

1.28 _true_ Cuneiform is a form of writing using wedge-shaped characters.

1.29 _false_ The clay tablets found at Ur told stories of poor leaders and military defeats.

1.30 _true_ These first libraries preserved records of Sumerian laws and religious music.

1.31 _true_ Mesopotamia was the "crossroads of the Middle East."

Complete these statements.

1.32 Two cities built by the Sumerians, other than Ur and Babylon, were
a. _Kish_ and b. _Nippur_ .

1.33 A great military leader in Babylon was _Hammurabi_ .

1.34 The Fertile Crescent was invaded by the _Hittites_ .

1.35 The two sections of Egypt were united by _Menes_ .

1.36 Egypt was ruled by powerful _Pharaohs_ .

1.37 Egypt's first capital city was _Memphis_ .

1.38 The Egyptians used a form of writing called _hieroglyphics writing_ .

1.39 The people who were expert sailors and traders in the Mediterranean area were the _Phoenicians_ .

1.40 Abraham went to Egypt during a _famine_ .

1.41 Abraham is recognized as the father of both the a. _Arabic_ and the b. _Hebrew_ nations.

Complete this activity.

1.42 On the outline map on page 10, write the names of the following ancient places in the correct locations. Use an atlas or an encyclopedia to find the correct locations.

- Egypt
- Canaan
- Jerusalem
- Nile River
- Phoenicia
- Ur
- Babylon
- Tigris River and Euphrates River
- Africa
- Mountains of Ararat

Teacher check _____

Initial   Date

9

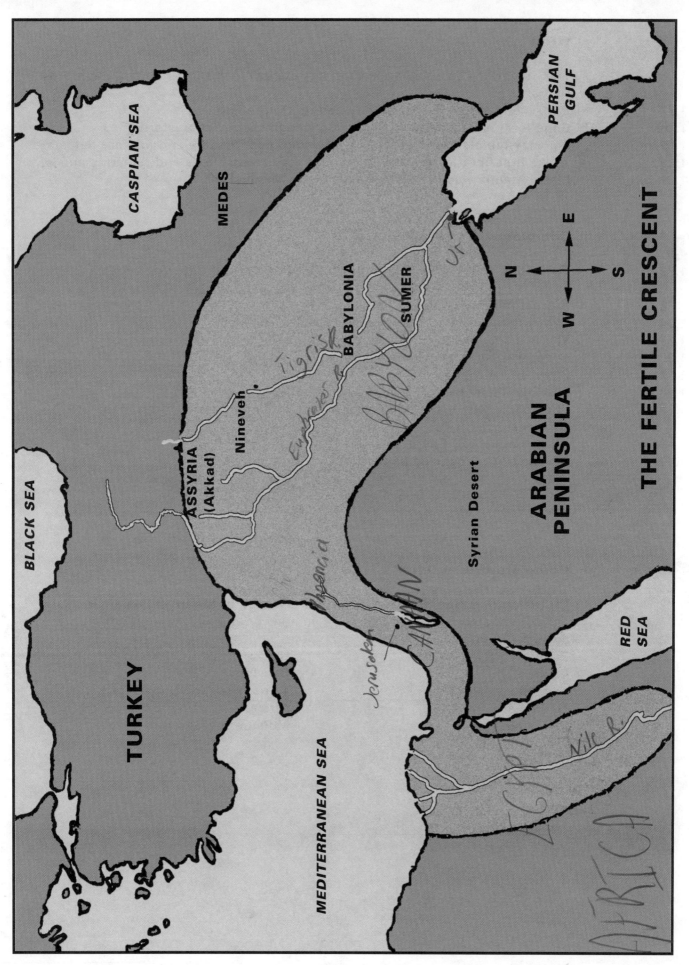

THE FERTILE CRESCENT

BLACK SEA

CASPIAN SEA

PERSIAN GULF

TURKEY

MEDES

ASSYRIA (Akkad)

Nineveh

Tigris R.

Euphrates R.

BABYLONIA

BABYLON

SUMER

Ur

MEDITERRANEAN SEA

Phoenicia

Jerusalem

CANAAN

Syrian Desert

ARABIAN PENINSULA

RED SEA

EGYPT

Nile R.

AFRICA

N W E S

Review the material in this section in preparation for the Self Test. The Self Test will check your mastery of this particular section. The items missed on this Self Test will indicate specific areas where restudy is needed for mastery.

SELF TEST 1

Put these events in proper order (each answer, 2 points).

1.01 _____5_____ The ark lands on Ararat.
1.02 _____8_____ The African continent is entered.
1.03 _____3_____ Man is removed from the garden.
1.04 _____1_____ God created heaven and earth.
1.05 _____9_____ Abraham leaves Ur.
1.06 _____10____ Abraham goes to Egypt.
1.07 _____4_____ The deluge begins.
1.08 _____6_____ Man begins building Babel.
1.09 _____7_____ Descendants of Ham head to Africa to live.
1.010 _____2_____ Adam and Eve are created.

Match the meanings with these words (each answer, 2 points).

1.011 ___c.___ petrify
1.012 ___i.___ fossil
1.013 ___j.___ fissure
1.014 ___a.___ antediluvian
1.015 ___b.___ papyrus
1.016 ___l.___ cuneiform
1.017 ___h.___ inundate
1.018 ___e.___ strata
1.019 ___d.___ tropical
1.020 ___f.___ silt
1.021 ___k.___ hieroglyphic

a. the period before the Flood
b. writing material can be made from this reed
c. to turn soft material into a stony substance
d. a place where lush vegetation grows in a warm climate
e. layers of rock or soil
f. fine particles of soil deposited by water
g. one who lives in or comes from Asia or the Far East
h. to flood or submerge under water
i. the preserved remains or the imprint of animal or plant life in rock
j. an opening or crack in the surface of the earth
k. Egyptian form of writing
l. Babylonian form of writing

Complete these statements (each answer, 3 points).

1.022 The area of the Fertile Crescent that lay between the Tigris and Euphrates rivers was known as _Mesopotamia_ .
1.023 The people who remained at Babel were the _Sumerians_ .
1.024 The first man's name was _Adam_ .
1.025 Because he was divinely created man actually belongs to _God_ .

11

1.026	A canopy of water once shielded man from *the sun's radiation*
1.027	The various layers of the earth are called *strata* .
1.028	One kind of fossil fuel is *ptrolenum* .

Match these items (each answer, 2 points).

1.029	g.	the ruler in ancient Egypt		a.	Babel
1.030	~~I.~~ H	a Sumerian of Mesopotamia		b.	Fertile Crescent
1.031	e.	united upper and lower Egypt		c.	"hothouse"
1.032	~~d.~~ C	the environment of early man		d.	Mesopotamia
1.03	b.	an arc-shaped area in the Middle East		e.	Menes
1.034	a.	the city and tower man began to build after the Flood		f.	Abraham
1.035	i.	Mediterranean sailors and traders		g.	Pharaoh
1.036	j.	a river, supported a civilization		h.	Ur
1.037	f.	the father of the Hebrew nation		i.	Phoenicians
1.038	d.	crossroads of the Middle East		j.	Nile
1.039	l.	Babylonian leader		k.	Memphis
				l.	Hammurabi

Answer these questions (each answer, 5 points).

1.040 How were fossil fuels formed? *During the Flood animals and plants got moved under the ground inside some places. These animals got old and they produced fuel. (Oil & coal)*

1.041 How would you describe the earth as it was before the Flood? *The earth was one large land mass, the earth had no polar regions, and the weather was spring-like. the climate was warm & humid. Soil was rich*

1.042 What changes took place in the earth's topography as a result of the Flood? *The earth had polar regions, it had mountain ranges it was not one large land mass, and it had place on the earth that had hot and cold (instead of one good temperature). chasms ope...*

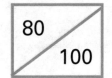

80 / 100

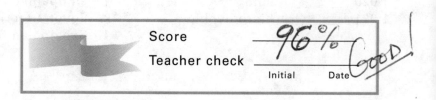

Score ___ 96% ___ GOOD!
Teacher check ___
Initial   Date

II. THE EARTH IS DEVELOPED BY MAN

After the Flood the earth's topography remained unsettled for a time. The Scriptures tell us (Genesis 8:2-3) that "The fountains also of the deep and the windows of heaven were stopped, and the rain from heaven was restrained; And the waters returned off the earth continually. . ."

The great ocean basins, hundreds of new and old underground river systems, both arctic regions, inland waters, and the atmosphere absorbed the waters of the Flood. Canyons, gorges, and deltas had been deepened or changed by the action of the receding waters. High mountain ranges grew more prominent as their foundations settled. Layers of soil dried and became solid strata of limestone, sandstone, and shale. New volcanic activity appeared in many places. Great barren plains that had been vast ocean beds were raked by strong wind currents. Before these areas were reseeded with plant life, the continual movement of wind-blown sand and the hot rays of the sun turned them into deserts. Flood-soaked tree trunks hardened into beautiful agatized petrified logs as minerals replaced rotting wood cells.

The earth was no longer at a perfect angle to the sun after the Flood. The original umbrella of water vapors had disappeared so that the sun's radiation now hit the earth's equator full force. However, at both north and south poles icy winds created great storms as drifting clouds loosed enormous snowfalls.

Large bodies of leftover inland water froze into glaciers. Later, as the earth's climate warmed, many of these first glaciers melted, leaving behind them a trail of evidence showing where they had been born.

Earth's constant spring-like climate was gone forever. Variable seasons were introduced to usher in new life. God promised man (Genesis 8:22), "While the earth remaineth, seedtime and harvest, and cold and heat, and summer and winter, and day and night shall not cease."

Man was now occupying a vastly altered earth. As man settled across its face, he saw he could improve his habitat in different ways. Curiously, man began studying the topography. He believed that if he could discover its new secrets, the earth would yield everything he would need for a rich full life.

In this section you will learn how civilization developed over the entire earth. You will study the development of water transportation systems, resources, and cities.

SECTION OBJECTIVES

Read these objectives to learn what you should be able to do when you have completed this section.

4. Describe when and how civilizations developed in different areas of the world.
5. Tell the contribution of navigation to the development of nations.
6. Tell the importance of the Industrial Revolution in shaping city life.
7. Outline urban problems as they developed in connection with labor and energy needs.
8. Identify how the environment is affected as man uses the natural resources.

VOCABULARY

Study these words to enhance your learning success in this section.

alloy (al'oi). A melting of two or more metals to create a new metal.

arable (ar' u bul). Capable of being plowed or cultivated.

corporation (kôr pu rā' shun). A group of people united to do business together.

dredge (drej). To scoop up and remove deposits that form in the bottom of a channel.

ductile (duk' tul). The ability for a metal to be drawn out into fine strands.

effluent (ef' lü unt). A mixture of liquid and solid sewage water.

fault (fôlt). Cracks or breaks in a body of rock with dislocation of the plane.

interdependent (in' tur di pen' dunt). Two or more things that depend on each other.

irrigate (ir' u gāt). To supply water to land by artificial means.

malleable (mal' ē u bul). The ability of a metal to be hammered into thin sheets.

outflow (out' flō'). That which flows from a river into an ocean, lake, or other body of water.

pitch (pich). A heavy thick oil used to seal the hulls of wooden ships.

refine (ri fīn'). To free from impurities and bring into a fine state.

sediment (sed'e ment). Rock formed by the deposit of matter.

slag (slag). Waste matter that is left after ore has been separated from it.

sludge (sluj). A deposit of thick waste slime that settles on river and lake bottoms.

smelt (smelt). To melt or fuse ore so that the metal contained in it can be separated.

urban (er' bun). Pertaining to city dwelling.

DEVELOPMENT OF CIVILIZATIONS

Civilization began to develop when man discovered that the raising of livestock and crops would provide a stable, adequate food supply. This discovery enabled groups of people to settle in villages as farmers and herdsmen. Man began to weave cloth, make pottery, and develop simple tools. As the villages grew, priests united the people in the worship of gods. Alliances were made between villages, and travelers and merchants were protected by chiefs. The peace and order that existed helped new ideas and trade to develop and spread.

The discovery of metals caused civilization to develop further. Metals were used for tools, weapons, and mediums of exchange. Systems of mathematics and writing were developed to keep records of trading activities. Wealth and trade led to a need for accounting.

Most of the world's great civilizations developed in temperate climates. The four oldest civilizations developed in the Eastern Hemisphere because of a plentiful food supply and easy transportation. The four centers of civilization were the Nile area of Egypt, the Mesopotamian area, the Indus valley, and the Hwang Ho valley of China.

Development of the Fertile Crescent. The Middle East includes a sickle-shaped area that curves from the Nile River northward around to the Persian Gulf. This very fertile region is known as the Fertile Crescent. The eastern part of this area was known as Mesopotamia, which lay between the Tigris and Euphrates rivers.

The ancient Egyptians lived along the banks of the Nile River. The Nile made transportation and travel easy. The Egyptians were able to grow wheat, rye, and other crops in the rich soil beside the Nile. The Egyptian villages were grouped in independent districts called nomes that dotted the river banks. These nomes were united into two kingdoms, Upper Egypt and Lower Egypt, and by 3000 B.C. Upper and Lower Egypt had united into one kingdom. Egyptian civilization continued for 2,500 years with little change. The Egyptians built great stone temples and pyramids, an indication of their concern with religion and with death. The Egyptians learned medical techniques of surgery and the development of drugs. They also invented a calendar and developed precise techniques of land measurement.

Abraham was a Hebrew who resided in Mesopotamia and went to Canaan about 2000 B.C. His descendants went into Egypt, possibly about 1650 B.C., and eventually became Egyptian slaves. Moses led the Hebrews out of Egyptian bondage and back to Canaan about 1250 B.C. The Hebrews were ruled by judges for about 300 years, but reached their greatest height during the reigns of King David and King Solomon. After the death of Solomon, the nation of Israel declined and went through a long series of bondages by the Assyrians, Persians, Babylonians, Chaldeans, Greeks, and Romans. The Hebrews' greatest contributions were the worship of the true and living God; the Bible, the Old and New Testaments; and many basic religious concepts known and used today.

The Phoenicians were a Semitic people who became prominent sometime prior to 3000 B.C. From 2000 B.C. to 1300 B.C., Phoenicia was under the control of Egypt. The Phoenicians were the first explorers, traders, and colonizers of the ancient world. They traded with Egypt about 3000 B.C. and by 1250 B.C. completely dominated Mediterranean trade. They explored and traded as far away as Spain, Britain, the Baltic Sea area, and around the Canary Islands in the Atlantic Ocean. The Phoenicians were thought to have circled the tip of Africa. The greatest contribution by the Phoenicians was the invention of a true alphabet, it consisted of twenty-one consonants to which the Greeks later added five vowels.

The Lydian culture had emerged by 700 B.C., and their greatest power was reached under King Croesus (560-546 B.C.). The most notable contribution of the Lydians was the invention of coined money as a regular medium of exchange. The Lydians were the first people to coin money as a government function (about 700 B.C.).

The Hittites were a nomadic Indo-European people who settled in Asia Minor about 2000 B.C. The old kingdom of the Hittites had a feudal aristocracy with the king crowned by the nobles. The Hittites were a warlike people who conquered northern Syria, drove the Hyksos into Egypt, and conquered the city of Babylon in 1590 B.C. The Hittite empire extended into much of Asia Minor, Syria, and northern Mesopotamia. The Hittites never attained a high cultural level as did other civilizations; however, they did develop iron **smelting**. They also produced iron weapons and used light, horse-drawn iron chariots in war. The Hittite empire collapsed soon after 1200 B.C.

The Assyrian empire began about 3000 B.C. in northeastern Mesopotamia. Because of the lack of natural protective barriers, the Assyrians were constantly under attack. The First Assyrian Empire (1310-1232 B.C.) had difficulty surviving. The Second Assyrian Empire (833-612 B.C.) was made a great military power under the leadership of some bold and capable kings. The Assyrian army was the first to be totally equipped with iron weapons. They were the first to develop new battle tactics using iron-tipped arrows in a heavy barrage followed by a charge of cavalry and heavy war chariots. The Assyrians perfected heavy siege equipment. They also introduced techniques of terrorization of enemies by burning entire cities and massacring or deporting entire populations. The Assyrians also had the most advanced administrative government up to that time. The absolute power of the monarchy was channeled through a highly centralized bureaucracy. They also introduced a postal service and the use of national highways.

The early Sumerians were building a civilization in Mesopotamia somewhat parallel to that of the Egyptians. The Sumerians grew wheat and raised cattle and sheep. They also worked metals brought from distant mines. Because of the absence of stone in the Mesopotamian area, palaces and temples were built of sun-dried brick. The Akkadians and Babylonians helped to spread Sumerian culture throughout Mesopotamia. The Sumerian culture was more widespread than the Egyptian culture, and it influenced several other cultures. The Sumerians used a seven-day week, the 360-degree circle, cuneiform writing, and large-scale **irrigation** systems.

The Babylonian civilization was founded about 2000 B.C. and was united as an empire by Hammurabi about 1792 B.C. Hammurabi developed a universal code of law that regulated society. This code included laws for (1) justice—several punishments based on the "eye-for-an-eye" principle; (2) family—marriage, divorce, and inheritance; and (3) business—labor, partnerships, and the introduction of commercial documents, such as wills and contracts. The code was based on class distinctions but with recognition of rights for women and for slaves. The Babylonians also developed observatories and a twelve-month lunar calendar. A system of mathematics was developed with solutions for algebraic and geometric problems. The Babylonian empire fell about 1590 B.C.

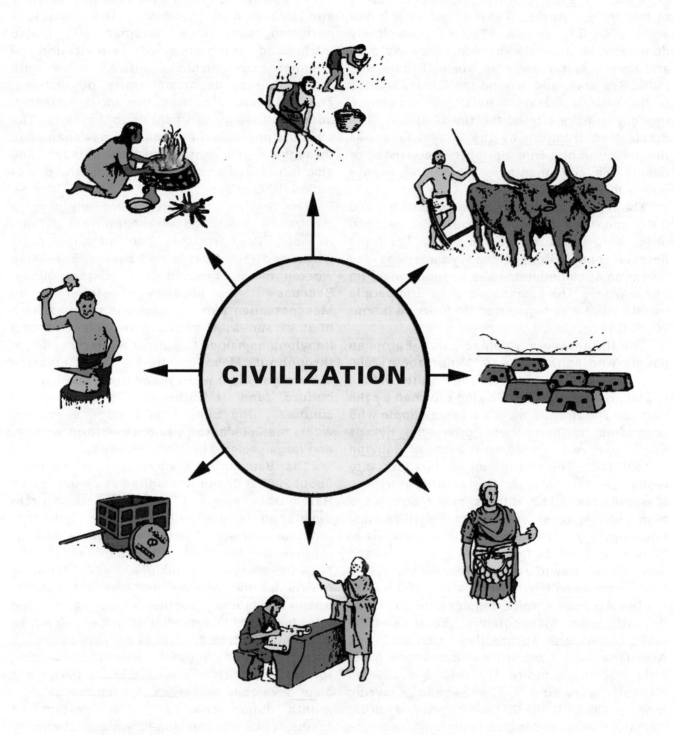

IMPORTANT EVENTS IN THE DEVELOPMENT OF CIVILIZATION

Match these items.

2.1	_c._	Nile River	a.	Babylonians
2.2	_c._	sun-dried bricks	b.	Lydians
2.3	_d._	skilled seamen	c.	Egyptians
2.4	_c._	seven-day week	d.	Phoenicians
2.5	_b._	coined money	e.	Sumerians
2.6	_c._	pyramids	f.	Hebrews
2.7	_f._	Bible	g.	Hittites
2.8	_a._	universal code of law	h.	Assyrians
2.9	_a._	calendar of twelve months		
2.10	_e._	cuneiform writing		
2.11	_d._	true alphabet		
2.12	_f._	worship of the living God		
2.13	_h._	iron weapons		
2.14	_h._	iron-tipped arrows		
2.15	_g._	horse-drawn chariots		
2.16	_h._	techniques of terrorism		
2.17	_h._	postal service		
2.18	_c._	surgery		

Development of European civilizations. The world's largest inland body of water is the Mediterranean Sea. The people who live along the Mediterranean's shores enjoy a mild climate and the ease of water transportation.

The earliest civilization along the Mediterranean and Aegean seas began around 300 B.C. The Minoans of Crete built beautiful cities, such as the city of Knossos, with extremely fine plumbing and fine wall paintings. The Minoans were good sailors and traders and spread their goods and civilization throughout the eastern Mediterranean area. The Minoan civilization that existed on the Greek mainland is often called the Mycenaean civilization. Its capital was at Mycenae.

The Greek civilization developed from a combination of cultures from the Aegean area and from foreign northern invaders. Greece reached its political height by mid 400 B.C. The Greeks used a true alphabet that was derived from the Egyptians through the Phoenicians. They also produced the first written works of history and science and developed the highest level of architecture and sculpture ever produced. The Greek concepts of democracy and justice have been used to form governments and policies of the Western civilizations.

Rome came to power during the early 400's B.C. Rome gradually extended its empire until it controlled the entire region from Britain to the Persian Gulf and from the Sahara Desert to northern Europe. The Romans combined cultural elements from the Etruscans, Greeks, Egyptians, and other civilizations, blending these into their own culture. Roman achievements included the construction of paved roads and aqueducts, the system of coded laws, and Latin. The collapse of the Roman Empire in A.D. 476 ended the period of ancient civilizations.

Complete these statements.

2.19 The largest inland body of water is the _Mediterranean sea_

2.20 The earliest civilization along the Mediterranean and Aegean seas was the _Minoans_ .

2.21 The city of Knossos was noted for its fine a. _plumbing_ and b. _wall paintings_ .

2.22 The Minoan civilization on the Greek mainland was called the _Mycenaean_ civilization.

2.23 The Greeks wrote a true alphabet that was derived from the a. _Egyptians_ through the b. _Phoenicians_ .

2.24 The Greeks produced the first written works of a. _history_ and b. _science_ .

2.25 Rome came to power during the early _400's BC_ B.C.

2.26 The Romans combined cultural elements from the a. _Etruscans_ , b. _Greeks_ , and c. _Egyptians_ .

2.27 Roman achievements included a. _paved roads_ , b. _a system of coded laws_ and c. _Latin_ . _(aqueducts)_

Development of Far Eastern civilizations. About 2500 B.C. a civilization began developing along the Indus River in Pakistan. The people of this civilization built cities, developed straight streets, and developed good drainage and sewer systems. The people worked with bronze, made fired bricks, and wrote with an alphabet that has yet to be deciphered. The people of the Indus valley traded with Mesopotamia and the surrounding regions. The Indus valley civilization collapsed around 1700 B.C.

The Hindu civilization in India developed out of a union of the Aryan culture with the earlier Indus-valley culture. India had frequently contained numerous tribes and nations. Because so many groups of people lived in one area, a caste system developed that defined a person's role in society. The Hindus have a well developed religious system, characterized by extensive religious lore and temples devoted to many gods and goddesses. The Hindus also used a numeral and decimal system derived from the Arabs.

A culture related to the Hindu civilization was the Khmer Empire of Cambodia. It flourished in the A.D. 800's. The Khmers built magnificent temples at Angkor Wat and at many other places.

About 1500 B.C. a civilization began along the Hwang Ho River in north-central China. These people cast the finest bronze utensils in the world. The Chinese used a highly developed system of writing. The Chinese also used iron and developed an iron-tipped, ox-drawn plow. The Great Wall was built during the Chin Dynasty, and during the Han Dynasty the Chinese developed movable type and gunpowder. Some of the most beautiful art in the world has come from China; porcelain, jade, silk and Chinese architecture have been appreciated by people from many cultures. The Chinese civilization has contributed many aspects of its culture to the Japanese and Korean civilizations.

Match these items.

2.28	_d._ Pakistan	a. Hindus
2.29	_c._ Angkor Wat	b. Chinese
2.30	_a._ decimal system	c. Khmers
2.31	_d._ straight streets	d. Indus valley
2.32	_b._ iron-tipped plow	
2.33	_a._ caste system	
2.34	_b._ movable type	
2.35	_b._ gunpowder	
2.36	_b._ porcelain	

Development of African civilization.
Farming skills and the use of animals to do man's work entered Africa from the Middle East. They quickly spread throughout North Africa and the region of the Sahara. At that time the Sahara in Africa was a fertile grassland.

By about twenty-five hundred years before Christ, a changing climate had turned the Sahara into the vast desert we know today. People who farmed there were forced to move south where they could continue to raise their crops. Before that time people south of the Sahara knew nothing about farming. Soon agriculture had spread into central Africa and as far east as Ethiopia.

An important group that entered central Africa about the time of Christ was the Bantu-speaking people. The Bantu-speakers were skilled in farming and in the use of iron. Hundreds of years passed, and these farmers expanded their control over the land until they occupied most of western Africa south to the Kalahari Desert. As their migration continued they encountered other tribes: Bushmen, Pygmies, and Hottentots. The Bantu-speakers either absorbed these peoples, intermarrying with them, or drove them into the rain forests and deserts to live. The Hottentots adopted the Bantu-speakers' culture and learned to live with them.

The culture of the Bantu-speakers was affected by their rapid migration. As they moved deeper into Africa, they moved away from the advanced civilization and new inventions of the Middle East. Nevertheless, the Bantu-speakers soon developed new ideas and inventions of their own.

Cities began to arise in North Africa about two thousand years before Christ. New inventions continued to be brought into Africa from the Middle East. Although the use of bronze was restricted to North Africa, iron technology spread through Egypt into the kingdom of Kush. Handwriting also was introduced from the Middle East and facilitated the developing sea trade of North Africa.

The great Roman Empire brought new trade routes across the Sahara and the Nile River valley. New trade brought new ideas and goods, especially those of Rome. Roman influence was greatest in Aksum and Nubia. Aksum became prosperous as a result of trade between the Romans and India. Eventually the people of Aksum became converts to Christianity and have remained so throughout history.

When Rome controlled Egypt, Nubian kingdoms along the Nile River maintained extensive trade there. About 500 A.D. the Nubians were also converted to Christianity.

For several hundreds of years, the strongest West African empire was Ghana; but as it declined, it was replaced in the 1200's by Mali in what is now Guinea. Mali was replaced later by Songhai as the seat of power in West Africa. During this time the kingdom of Kongo, at the mouth of the Congo River in Angola, was the largest political empire in South Africa. The Lubas also were a South African empire.

➡️ **Complete these lists.**

2.37 List five civilizations that developed in Africa other than the Egyptians.
a. *Bantu-speaking people (Bantus)*
b. *Rome Ethiopia*
c. *Nubian people*
d. *Bushmen Kongo*
e. *Pygmies Hottentots, Mali, Ghana, Aksum, Lubas*

2.38 Name two ways the Bantu speakers treated the groups they encountered.
a. *they intermarried them* ✓
b. *they drove them into the rain forests and deserts*

Development of Western civilizations. Several groups of Indians in both North America and South America attained a high degree of civilization. These Indians lacked beasts of burden and the wheel. Neither their cities nor their writing systems developed in the same way as those of the Middle East, Asia, and Egypt. However, the Indians made great advances before the coming of the Europeans in the A.D. 1500's. Some tribes built large cities around their temples or pyramids.

The Incas, who lived in the Andes Mountains of South America, began developing advanced ways of living about A.D. 400. The Incas grew potatoes, beans, maize, and quinoa. The Incas domesticated the llama and the guinea pig. They invented bronze and cast many beautiful objects of gold and silver. The Incas wove intricate cloth of cotton and wool. They built large walls without the use of mortar, and those walls remain today. The Incas paved roads and built suspension bridges across large gorges. During the 1400's the Incas united a large region into a single empire.

In Guatemala, Honduras, and the Yucatan Peninsula, the Mayan civilization arose. The Mayan culture reached its height in the A.D. 700's. The people built beautiful limestone temples and produced fine paintings, sculpture, and pottery. The Mayans invented a calendar system based on the movement of the sun, the moon, and the planet Venus. They developed a hieroglyphic writing system, the mathematical concepts of zero, and the place-value system.

While the Mayans were developing in Central America, the Aztecs were developing a great civilization in the valley of Mexico. The Aztecs were primarily agriculturalists. They also built stone pyramids, worked in metal, and traded throughout Mexico and possibly as far east as the central United States.

Match these items.

2.39	b.	Andes Mountains	a. Incas
2.40	b.	Guatemala	b. Mayans
2.41	c.	Mexico	c. Aztecs
2.42	c.	trade in United States	
2.43	a.	invented bronze	
2.44	b.	calendar system	
2.45	b.	limestone temples	
2.46	a.	llama	
2.47	c.	stone pyramids	

DEVELOPMENT OF WATER TRANSPORTATION SYSTEMS

Navigation was probably not widely practiced before the Flood. Noah's experience proved to all future generations that travel by boat was possible and safe. Thus, when man dispersed from Babel, he knew that he could get to some places easier and faster by water craft.

The earliest boats were of simple construction. These boats were most likely hollowed-out logs, rafts, or crude canoes. Primitive cargoes would consist of only a few people with their meager possessions. Many ancient seacoast villagers obviously developed small fishing craft from which to harvest marine life from the nearby waters.

Large seaworthy vessels were made by the Phoenicians and were equipped with oars and with sails. They were used on trading expeditions among Middle Eastern countries as early as 2000 B.C. Timber from the vast forests of Lebanon and **pitch** were traded to Egypt for gold crafts and other merchandise. The Phoenicians were subjects of Egypt for a brief period of time, but by 1200 B.C. they had become independent city-states again. To guard their treasures from trading expeditions, they built warships with pointed bows. They used these primitive destroyers to ram their enemies' vessels. By 900 B.C. King David of Israel and Solomon, his son, were trading heavily with the Phoenicians. Solomon purchased cedar so that a beautiful palace and the Lord's Temple could be constructed in Jerusalem.

The Phoenicians established trade cities around the entire rim of the Mediterranean and are believed to have sailed around Africa and to the British Isles with their wares. The Carthaginians and Greeks borrowed most of their navigational knowledge from these expert seamen. Two of the Phoenician home ports were Tyre and Sidon. The prophet Ezekiel foretold the ruin of these proud cities in Ezekiel, Chapters 27 and 28.

Sailors on the Pacific side of the world also had sea-faring skills and explored and settled many islands near their continental homeland. Some of these Asiatics had not reckoned with strong oceans tides and were cast upon strange shores. As time passed, they developed new cultures. Thus, a variety of cultures began flourishing in remote areas, accessible only by water craft. The mainland Chinese eventually invented a compass with which to safely guide their fishermen and sea explorers home.

As man began to discover and share new navigational aids, such as the astrolabe, he became more certain that he would return to his home port after a long journey. One such ship that did not return to its Scandinavian home was captained by Leif Erickson. This great explorer is known to have explored the shores and waterways of North America as early as A.D. 1000. He was representative of the fierce Vikings of Norway and Denmark who colonized Greenland and plundered many European shore villages.

Mariners everywhere were restricted to the use of the oar and sail until steam power was discovered by Robert Fulton in 1814. Progressive nations began immediately replacing their sails with boilers and smokestacks. New and deeper mines were opened in Europe to provide coal for these larger merchant ships and warships. The age of steam guaranteed that ships would not be at the mercy of contrary winds.

Before the advent of steam, many fierce battles were fought on the high seas by nations that wanted to control the rich sea-lane trade. Pirates were also a threat to shipping after the Americas were discovered. From the sixteenth to the nineteenth centuries, many battles were fought from the decks of numerous men-of-war. When a colony would demand independence from its mother country, victories at sea would sometimes determine if the revolution would succeed.

Merchants pressed their governments to employ engineers to find ways of cutting the cost of long-distance shipping. Long canals to connect rivers with larger bodies of water were started by engineering companies. Eventually, even oceans were flowing together through the locks of wide, modern canals, such as the Panama and Suez canal. People also discovered that **dredging** shallow rivers would allow inland cities to have ports.

Ship turbines burning fossils fuels soon replaced coal-powered steam vessels. With the start of World War II, several powerful navies had already developed diesel-powered ships.

Then, the atomic age introduced nuclear energy to the field of navigation. However, only the most advanced nations can afford this type of propulsion.

Development of Water Transportation

Write *true* **or** *false.*

2.48 _false_ Sea navigation was widely practiced before the Flood.
2.49 _true_ The earliest boats were hollowed-out logs, rafts, or crude canoes.
2.50 _true_ Large seaworthy vessels first appeared in the Mediterranean.
2.51 _true_ The first nation to trade by sea was Phoenicia, as early as 2000 B.C.
2.52 _false_ Egypt was the first nation to use warships.
2.53 _true_ King David of Israel traded with the Phoenicians.

Complete these sentences.

2.54 Two Phoenician home ports were a. _Tyre_ and
b. _Sidon_ .

2.55 Most of the navigational knowledge of the a. _Carthaginians_ and
b. _Greeks_ was borrowed from the Phoenicians.

2.56 The Chinese invented the _compass_ to safely guide their fishermen
and explorers.

2.57 The Viking explorer who reached North America about A.D. 1000 was
Leif Erickson.

2.58 The steamboat was invented by _Robert Fulton_

2.59 Rivers and oceans were connected to one another by the use of
canals .

2.60 Two famous canals that connected oceans and seas are the
a. _Panama_ and b. _Suez_

2.61 To make shallow rivers deeper a process called _dredging_ is used.

2.62 Two fuels that power modern ships are a. _diesel_ and
b. _coal nuclear (atomic)_

2.63 Until the discovery of steam power, ships were moved by either a.
oars or b. _sails_ .

DEVELOPMENT OF RESOURCES

The Scriptures state that some precious minerals were plentiful in prehistoric times (Genesis 2:11, 12): ". . .there is gold; and the gold of that land [Havilah] is good: there is bdellium and the onyx stone." Possibly during the Flood, such mineral deposits that had originally been easy to find were washed into **faults**; mixed with soil, rock, and other minerals; and scattered everywhere. Noah's descendants had to seek such minerals by the sweat of their brows.

Gold is so **malleable** that it can be beaten into leaves so thin that 200,000 leaves would make a stack one inch high. Gold is so **ductile** that if all that had been discovered during the past five hundred years could be pulled into a wire, it would stretch more than one hundred billion miles into space.

Gold, as well as silver, is found in copper deposits. Enough gold is found in some copper mines to finance the entire cost of producing and **refining** the copper. Thus, the copper and other minerals can be sold for pure profit. Gold is also found in soluble form in ocean water. However, the process of separating the one grain of gold from a ton of sea water is currently too expensive.

The Sumerians, Egyptians, and other early civilizations worked with gold and copper. The Chinese, Incas, and American Indian tribes also learned to work with these metals. **Smelting** was introduced about 3500 B.C. in the Middle East. Five hundred years later copper was **alloyed** with tin to produce bronze. Brass is a blend of copper and zinc and was widely used from about 1000 B.C. until 600 B.C. These metals and others were easy to locate during the first few thousand years of man's history, so the earth was left comparatively unscarred by miners. During the Dark Ages, mining in Europe almost became a lost art. However, the Industrial Revolution created a tremendous demand for metals of various kinds.

Early in this century an American, Daniel Jackling, introduced the idea of open-pit mining. Huge steam shovels were built and tons of top soil were quickly removed from known low-grade mineral deposits. Coal veins that stretched across the hills and valleys of Kentucky, West Virginia, Illinois, Pennsylvania, and other areas in the United States were opened and stripped of many tons of fossil fuel.

Many geological mining expeditions have been organized in recent years. Geologists, chemists and geophysicists are now employed by mining concerns to find hidden minerals. Satellites equipped with special cameras to locate secret deposits of metal-bearing ores are being used today around the world.

The disposal of the waste and **slag** from mining operations did not cause much concern to the first mine owners. To cut their disposal costs, owners dumped their deadly mine acids into nearby streams and rivers. Fish and other marine life died. These waterways would occasionally overflow and leave behind them barren and unproductive land. Thus, thousands of acres of land have been spoiled by mining and drilling in the United States alone.

Only in recent years have citizens of manufacturing nations begun to demand that controls be placed on the disposal of wastes from mining and from related industries. In the United States the Environmental Protection Agency was created to police the companies causing pollution problems. The real answer, however, lies with an informed citizenry that will minimize and reverse the destruction of their landscape. With the scientific knowledge that man now possesses, he can find solutions to the pollution problem.

Write the letter for the correct choice.

2.64 The most precious metal on earth is _____ b. _____ .
a. silver   c. copper
b. gold   d. iron

2.65 Gold can be beaten into leaves so thin that _____ d. _____ leaves would make a stack one inch high.
a. 60,000   c. 1,020,000
b. 300,000   d. 200,000

2.66 Gold and silver can be found in _____ a. _____ deposits.
a. copper   c. iron
b. quartz   d. nickel

2.67 Smelting was introduced about 3500 B.C. in _____ a. _____ .
a. the Middle East   c. Greece
b. Egypt   d. India

2.68 About 3000 B.C. copper was alloyed with tin to produce _____ c. _____ .
a. brass   c. bronze
b. nickel   d. chrome

2.69 The blend of copper and zinc is called _____ b. _____ .
a. chrome   c. bronze
b. brass   d. nickel

2.70 Daniel Jackling introduced the idea of _____ d. _____ mining.
a. strip   c. drift
b. quarry   d. open-pit

2.71 Describe how open-pit mines could be renovated so that future generations could enjoy mining-country topography.

We could make an open-pit mine in a smaller area and go deeper instead of going shallow over a wide area.

Teacher check _____

Initial   Date

DEVELOPMENT OF CITIES

Ur, a city of the ancient Chaldees in Mesopotamia, was the home of more than 30,000 citizens. Such a concentration of people created a large demand for food, fuel, housing, and other needs. Securing food was not a difficult task. The great silted plains of the Fertile Crescent were irrigated to provide enough food for Ur, and possibly surplus food was shipped out to other settlements situated in the valley. The nearby Euphrates River provided a liquid highway for transporting farm produce from field to city and beyond.

By 3000 B.C. settlements that would later grow into cities had been planted along the Nile. The Indus valley also hosted urban communities as early as 2500 B.C. Five hundred years later the Chinese had created centers for commerce in the Hwang Ho River valley. The Indians of North America formed their first cities around pyramidal temples of worship. The height of their urban culture emerged around 500 A.D. Thus, man began to organize his scattered rural communities into more effective groups of **interdependent** societies; and the world's first cities were given birth.

In this section you will learn how the Industrial Revolution caused the growth of cities. You will also discover the importance of technology and the problems of pollution.

Development of the Industrial Revolution. Historians say that prior to the 1800's only one city in the world ever reached a population of a million people. Rome, the capital of an empire that controlled 50 million people, has this lone distinction.

During medieval times cities everywhere in Europe experienced a serious decline in population. Even Rome's multitude of citizens had dwindled to about 20,000 in number.

When the feudal system began to break down, urban centers could hardly keep pace with the growth, as serfs moved from the manors to the revived cities. By A.D. 1600 London and Paris hosted a half million inhabitants each. People were relocating into cities for a variety of reasons. The availability of jobs, other than hard farm labor, drew many men. Easier access to religious, cultural, and recreational activities brought others in. The movement of neighbors looking for a better way of life tempted some families to also consider relocating in a city. Seaports boomed as thousands of European emigrants booked passage for the New World. Cities in the Western Hemisphere quickly grew as immigrants continued to enter the area looking for a better life.

England was the first nation to profit from the Industrial Revolution. England's energetic government and military leaders knew that their country controlled the seas. Loyal British administrators established colonial cities around the world. The United States, Canada, India, and some African nations can trace their economic beginnings to a brisk trade with England.

England was a leader in the development of transportation and communication. By 1800 England had built a vast network of canals to freight wares to and from world markets. The first turnpike was constructed in England so that merchants could move quickly overland to the city to conduct their business. The first British railroad was opened in 1825. Other European nations quickly developed railway systems of their own. By 1866, only twenty-two years after the telegraph had been invented, a transatlantic cable had been stretched from the United States to England, and intercontinental telegraph lines could be found between numerous cities on both continents. Such rapid transportation and communication changes drastically affected the shipment of goods to world markets.

With the arrival of the machine age, governments began looking for additional sources of energy to use in developing cities and their interdependent industries. Great rivers were harnessed to provide hydroelectric power. Aqueducts, similar to those used by the Romans, were constructed so that the reservoirs behind the dams could be used to store and supply water to meet the needs of a nation's people. Irrigation systems were introduced so that land would be **arable** enough to grow crops in drier climates of the world. These water engineering projects enable desert cities like Phoenix, Arizona, for example, to experience tremendous population growth.

Living conditions in industrial cities were very difficult. Tens of thousands of city dwellers, including children, were recruited to labor long hours in all types of factories for low wages. Some cities were overrun with disease-ridden rats and lice. Plagues decimated city populations. Crime of every sort flourished even though severe penalties awaited law-breakers. Raw sewage openly flowed through streets and clogged rivers that rolled sluggishly toward **outflows** in the ocean. Thick smog from numerous smokestacks and chimneys saturated the air, remaining like a black cloud over the cities' skylines.

Industrial cities of 200 years ago survived these crises; and many have become busy, important metropolitan centers. Some of their problems, however, have continued into modern times and burden the **urban** residents of today.

Write the letter of the correct answer.

2.72   The largest city before modern times was ___ a. ___ .
        a. Rome, during the Roman Empire   c. Paris, before A.D. 1600
        b. Ur, after 4000 B.C.

2.73   The nation that profited most from the Industrial Revolution was ___ c. ___ .
        a. Greece   c. England
        b. Russia

2.74   During medieval times, the population of European cities ___ b. ___ .
        a. boomed   c. moved
        b. declined   d. disappeared

Answer these questions.

2.75   What were three reasons cities grew during the Late Middle Ages?
        a. _the availability of jobs_
        b. _easier access to Religious cultural, and recreational activities_
        c. _because some people decided to go because their neighbors._
        c. breakdown of feudal system or looking for better way of life.

26

2.76　　　　What three nations had their economic beginnings through trade with Great Britain?
　　　　a.　*United States* ✓
　　　　b.　*Canada* ✓
　　　　c.　*India* ✓

2.77　　　　What were three ways goods could be shipped quickly?
　　　　a.　*canals* ✓
　　　　b.　*the turnpike* ✓
　　　　c.　*the railroad* ✓

2.78　　　　What were two ways desert areas could get necessary water?
　　　　a.　*aqueducts* ✓
　　　　b.　*using rivers*　*dams, irrigation*

Complete this activity.

2.79　　　　Write a three-page report on the living conditions in the cities during the 1800's or early 1900's in the United States. Use at least two sources including an encyclopedia for your information. Have your teacher check your report before you read it to the class. You may want to report on a particular city in the United States.

Teacher check _____

　　　　　　　　　　　　　　　　Initial　　　　　　　　　　　Date

Development of technology. If man still depended on hunting to provide his major source for food, the world could only support a total population of a few million people. By subduing the earth to grow food crops and to develop its other natural resources, man expanded the limits of his population growth.

The rise and fall of civilizations throughout history and the emergence of cities and nations had little effect on the earth's tremendous store of resources. However, the Industrial Revolution applied pressure to the development of these gifts God had preserved for man. From the beginning of the nineteenth century, science and technology have been harnessed to help man find the raw materials provided in the earth that he could use. Coal and petroleum began to be used for fuel to energize power-driven machines to manufacture every kind of product man needed in life. The coming of the machine age demanded that new markets be located close to transportation routes. Profits from the sale of merchandise made governments, as well as individual families, prosperous. Wealthy men from Western nations traveled broadly with their manufacturing concerns. Groups of wealthy businessmen created **corporations** to meet a world-wide demand for more goods. To facilitate transportation, governments engineered intercontinental road systems. As industry expanded, deeper mines were dug, more oil wells were drilled, and larger factories were built. However, waterways, oceans, landscapes, and airways had a limit to the demand that the development of industry placed upon them. The environment in some metropolitan areas of the world was soon overtaxed.

Development of pollution. Ecology is the study of living organisms in relationship to their environment. Every one of God's creatures has its own niche to fill on earth. Man was given dominion over the earth and all of its creatures. However, man also has the responsibility to clean up the environment after he has taken what he needs from the earth.

Man has not always managed his environment in a proper way. For example, earth's waterways have been greatly abused. Modern man continues to mistreat these gifts of creation by overloading their carrying capacities. If an excessive amount of **effluent** is pumped into a river, the waterway becomes a long, polluted sewer. The river's bottom, coated with thick **sludge**, can no longer support fish or other aquatic life. Even the vast oceans can absorb only a limited amount of waste before their systems begin to break down.

The great metropolitan area of Chicago, Illinois, produces more than 1,000 tons of effluent daily. Engineers learned that the Great Lakes could not handle such a waste load. About one half of Chicago's sludge is currently being dried and shipped to Florida where it is sold to fruit growers. These growers use it to fertilize their citrus orchards. A suggestion has been made to ship the remaining one half to central Illinois where it could be used as landfill. This would restore the landscape that strip mining has scarred. These methods of disposal are known to conservationist as waste reuse.

For many years man practiced waste transfer. He dumped every kind of pollutant into nearby waterways to be carried downstream or into the airways to be blown downwind to the next city. This action only postponed the solution to the disposal problem and did not solve it.

Polluting Our Waterways

The use of air currents to carry pollutants into the sky has overtaxed some of earth's airsheds. Man has actually endangered his own species in some areas by discharging many poisons into the atmosphere.

One main cause of air pollution is the use of fossil fuels for generating electricity and for operating automobiles. Before environmental controls were established, United States citizens were emitting 2 million tons of lead from their automobile exhausts into their air space annually.

The use of coal to provide energy for this nation is an even greater pollution threat. To correct this problem, scientists are learning to gasify coal so that less sulphur dioxide will enter the air streams when the fuel burns.

Discharging fumes, toxic pesticides, smoke, and other emissions into the air can change local weather patterns. For example, Chicago received seven more inches of rain during a certain ten-year period than surrounding areas because its heavy smog affected the atmosphere above the city.

Modern man must also find new ways to dispose of his daily garbage. In the United States an average of nearly two thousand pounds of junk and trash per person is discharged annually. City dumps cannot continue to receive such loads. Some recycling of refuse, such as metal, glass, and paper, is being done. Such efforts are helpful, but more action needs to be taken to ensure that waste reuse is practiced everywhere. Otherwise, the United States and other advanced nations may soon become gigantic garbage heaps.

Complete these statements.

2.80   Before the use of electricity, power-driven machinery was fueled by
        a. _fossil fuel petroleum_ or b. _coal_ .

2.81   Thick sewage that settles on the bottom of rivers and lakes is called
        sludge .

2.82   _Ecology_ is _the study of living organisms in relationship to their environment_ .

Answer these questions.

2.83 What is the meaning of waste transfer? _getting rid of waste by dumping it into rivers or blowing in somewhere else; and making it someone else's problem._

2.84 What could good waste reuse habits mean to Americans? _It would mean we would be cleaner and it would prevent us from becoming a giant pile of garbage._

_____

_____

_____

Review the material in this section in preparation for the Self Test. This Self Test will check your mastery of this particular section as well as your knowledge of the previous section.

SELF TEST 2

Write the letter for the correct choice (each answer, 2 points).

2.01 The earliest city in history to total 1 million citizens in population was ___b.___ .
  a. London   c. Paris
  b. Rome

2.02 Finding enough land for growing food was no problem for the ___a.___ .
  a. Mesopotamians   c. Cretans
  b. modern Japanese

2.03 During the nineteenth century, emigrants flocked from European countries to the Western Hemisphere country of ___c.___ .
  a. South Africa   c. the United States
  b. Brazil

2.04 American Indians built their largest city cultures around ___a.___ .
  a. temple pyramids   c. castles and moats
  b. cliff dwellings

2.05 Smelting of metal ores was first practiced in ___a.___ .
  a. the Middle East   c. Japan
  b. Mexico

2.06 The person who first introduced the idea of open-pit mining was ___c.___ .
  a. Robert Fulton   c. Daniel Jackling
  b. Robert Stephenson

2.07   Copper is alloyed with tin to produce __b.__ ✓.
        a. brass   c. turquoise
        b. bronze   d. zinc
2.08   A threat to colonial shipping came from __c.__ ✓.
        a. the Phoenicians   c. pirates
        b. Nazi U-boats
2.09   The largest island of Greece is __a.__ ✓.
        a. Crete   c. Scandinavia
        b. Ararat
2.010   The first Mediterranean mariner/merchants were the __a.__ ✓.
        a. Phoenicians   c. Egyptians
        b. Hebrews

Match these items (each answer, 2 points).
2.011   __g.__ ✓ papyrus   a. rock formed by the deposit of matter
2.012   __k.__ ✓ coal   b. Babylonian form of writing
2.013   __a.__ ✓ sedimentary   c. ruler of ancient Egypt
2.014   __i.__ ✓ hieroglyphic   d. crack running across the earth's surface
2.015   __f.__ ✓ strata   e. father of the Hebrew nations
2.016   __c.__ ✓ Pharaoh   f. layers of the earth
2.017   __b.__ ✓ cuneiform   g. writing material made from reeds
2.018   __j.__ ✓ petroleum   h. flood or submerge under water
2.019   __d.__ ✓ fissure   i. Egyptian form of writing
2.020   __e.__ ✓ Abraham   j. formed from animals buried in the Flood
                                   k. formed from plants buried in the Flood

Complete these statements (each answer, 3 points).
2.021   Two types of fossil fuel are a. _petroleum_ ✓ and
        b. _coal_ ✓.
2.022   The atomic age introduced what is known as ~~atomic~~ _nuclear_ energy.
2.023   The preserved animal or plant life remains or imprints found in rocks are
        called _fossils_ ✓ (replenish or subdue)
2.024   ½ God told man to _populate_ (replenish subdue) the earth.
2.025   The ark carrying Noah and his family landed on Mt. a. _Arat_ Ararat
        in b. ~~Iran~~ _Turkey_.
2.026   The first civilization to coin money was the _Lydians_ ✓.
2.027   The postal system was first used by the _Assyrians_ ✓.
2.028   The worship of God and the Bible were _Hebrew_ ✓ contributions.
2.029   Porcelain works came from the _Chinese_ ✓.
2.030   A calendar based on the sun, moon, and Venus was used by the
        ~~Egyptians~~ _Mayans_
2.031   The Inca Indians lived in the a. ~~Rocky~~ _Andes_ Mountains of b.
        South America.

2.032	Trade was carried on in parts of the United States by the _Aztek_ ✓ Indians.
2.033	Two instruments developed to aid travelers at sea were the a. _compass_ ✓ and the b. ~~sextant~~ _astrolabe_ ✓
2.34	Two famous canals that connect oceans and seas are the a. _Panamal_ ✓ and the b. _Suez_ ✓ .

Write *true* **or** *false* (each answer, 1 point).

2.035 _true_ ✓ The study of living organisms in relationship to their environment is *ecology*.

2.036 _true_ ✓ Letting a waterway carry untreated raw sewage downstream is called waste transfer.

2.037 _true_ ✓ Recycling aluminum cans is one example of waste reuse.

Match these items (each answer, 3 points).

2.038 _c._ ✓ linguistic

2.039 _d._ ✓ arable

2.040 _e._ ✓ urban

2.041 _a._ ✓ irrigate

2.042 _b._ ✓ corporation

a. To supply water to land by artificial means
b. A group of people organized for business purpose
c. Having to do with different languages
d. Able to be cultivated
e. City dwelling

| 80 / 100 | | Score _88%_ Teacher check _(initialed)_ Initial   Date |

III. THE EARTH HAS A FUTURE

Just prior to the Flood the Lord told Noah (Genesis 6:13), ". . .The end of all flesh is come before me; for the earth is filled with violence through them; and , behold, I will destroy them with the earth." More than two thousand years later Jesus Christ stated (Luke 17:26-27), "And as it was in the days of Noe [Noah], so shall it be also in the days of the Son of man. They did eat, they drank, they married wives, they were given in marriage, until the day the Noe entered into the ark, and the flood came, and destroyed them all."

According to numerous Scripture references, mankind is approaching a period in time when he can expect some world shattering events to happen. Jesus taught that many signs would show that a judgment day was approaching. Yet, people will be so occupied in selfish and violent pursuits that they will be completely caught off guard. Concerning the end time, Jesus said these words (Matthew 24:5-14):

. . .Many shall come in my name, saying, I am Christ; and shall deceive many. And ye shall hear of wars and rumours of wars. . . For nation shall rise against nation, and kingdom against kingdom: and there shall be famines, and pestilences, and earthquakes, in divers places. . . Then shall they deliver you up to be afflicted, and shall kill you: and ye shall be hated of all nations for my name's sake. And then shall many be offended, and shall betray one another, and shall hate one another. And many false prophets shall rise, and shall deceive many. And because iniquity shall abound, the love of many shall wax cold. . . And this gospel of the kingdom shall be preached in all the world for a witness unto all nations; and then shall the end come.

In this section you will study the future of the earth. You will examine the efforts of world leaders in their pursuit of world peace, and you will learn about the divine judgment that will culminate in a universal peace.

SECTION OBJECTIVES

Read these objectives to learn what you should be able to do when you have completed this section.

    9.   Describe the events that will prepare the world for an evil world rule.

    10.   Explain what will happen to earth and man's civilization when Christ comes to judge the world.

    11.   Describe how God is preparing man for his external habitat.

VOCABULARY

Study these words to enhance your learning success in this section.

Antichrist (an' ti krīst'). The false messiah; the antagonist of Jesus Christ who pretends to be the promised redeemer.

Armageddon (är' mu ged' un). The place where a great final battle between the forces of good and evil will be fought.

cataclysm (kat' u kliz' um). Any violent change or upheaval.

catastrophe (ku tas' tru fē). A sudden disaster, a cataclysm.

imminent (im' u nunt). About to happen; impending.

millennium (mu len' ē um). A period of one thousand years in length.

symbolize (sim' bu līz). To represent something with a type of a figure.

vial (vī' ul). A symbolic vessel from which judgment or vengeance can be poured forth.

WORLD LEADERS PURSUE PEACE

The Apostle Paul wrote (I Thessalonians 5:1-3), "But of the times and seasons, brethren, ye have no need that I write unto you. For yourselves know perfectly that the day of the Lord so cometh as a thief in the night. For when they shall say, Peace and safety; then sudden destruction cometh upon them, as travail upon a woman with child; and they shall not escape."

World peace has always proved to be elusive to man. Agreements have been signed to limit war and arms build-ups, only to be followed by another conflict or rehearsal for war. Man appears to be unable to control his hostilities and aggression. One historian has figured that for every year of peace, mankind has endured ten years of war. Although the United States has only been involved in about a dozen wars in its brief history, other major nations have not been so fortunate. During the past two centuries, England has been engaged in seventy conflicts; Russia has fought more than sixty; and Austria has fought fifty wars.

Spain has fought in sixty wars over the past 200 years, and other European countries have fought more than twenty wars each.

Wars normally last for years. However, one war lasted only a few minutes. In 1896 Zanzibar declared war on Great Britain. Six English warships were stationed in Zanzibar's harbor when war was declared. The ships immediately opened fire on the Sultan's palace, killing 500 of his soldiers. The Sultan sued for peace. Thus, this shortest of all wars lasted only thirty-seven minutes and twenty-three seconds.

Modern wars have been very costly. During World War II, 54 million people perished; 7 million of them were Germans. Six million casualties in that war were Jews; and millions more were noncombatant men, women, and children. During World War I, seventeen nations spent $337 billion for the war efforts. More than 8 million lives were lost. War also wastes the land and its natural resources; it drains a nation's health and productivity.

Soon after World War I, the League of Nations was founded. This international association of countries was created to settle quarrels between nations. The United States did not join the League of Nations. The League's greatest failure came in 1935 when it could not prevent Italy from invading Ethiopia.

Following World War II, the United States and more than one hundred other nations founded a new world organization called the United Nations. The United Nations charter pledges its membership "to practice tolerance and to live in peace with one another as good neighbors." Unlike the League of Nations, the United Nations does not require all its members to agree to preserve national boundaries. The United Nations can recommend action, but it cannot order full participation by its membership. The major work of the United Nations is political, economic, and social. Its members can join together militarily to intervene if they see an unjust struggle taking place between nations.

Peacekeeping by diplomacy seems necessary as man seeks ways to curb his neighbor's greed and violence. Jesus said (Matthew 5:9), "Blessed are the peacemakers: for they shall be called the children of God."

Return of world government. World leaders recognize that some nations are capable of destroying one another with their arsenal of sophisticated weapons. Most national leaders ignore the truth that Jesus Christ can bring peace through His Gospel. By rejecting God's Son, man is deceived into thinking that his own human resources can provide solutions to his sin and destructiveness. Many people hope that a great statesman will soon arise who has abilities and unusual wisdom to lead the world community into a period of peace and prosperity.

The Apostle Paul warned the Thessalonians about a powerful world ruler to come (II Thessalonians 2:4 and 9): ". . .He as God sitteth in the temple of God, shewing himself that he is God. . .whose coming is after the working of Satan with all power and signs and lying wonders." This powerful **Antichrist** will take firm control of world affairs and will

34

demonstrate his great power to the world. Revelation 13:13, 16, and 17 records that "...he doeth great wonders, so that he maketh fire come down from heaven on the earth in the sight of men. . .and he causeth all, both small and great, rich and poor, free and bond, to receive a mark in their right hand, or in their foreheads: And that no man might buy or sell, save he that had the mark, or the name of the beast, or the number of his name."

Noah and his family were saved from the Flood because of the ark. Christians can rely on Christ to deliver them from the judgments that face an ungodly world system led by Antichrist. The Apostle Paul wrote (I Corinthians 2:9), "But as it is written, Eye hath not seen, nor ear heard, neither have entered into the heart of man, the things which God hath prepared for them that love him."

Return of Jesus Christ. When Jesus Christ returns to earth to claim His rightful rule, a great war will be fought. This war is often called the battle of **Armageddon**. Christ will put an end to the seven-year reign of the Antichrist. Christians may differ in their opinions as to the order in which the events of the end time will take place. However, most Christians agree that Jesus will return to earth to rule and to reign.

At Christ's Ascension the promise was made to his disciples (Acts 1:11) that, "...this same Jesus, which is taken up from you into heaven, shall so come in like manner as ye have seen him go into heaven." The blessed hope of Christ's **imminent** return gave His disciples courage to publish His Gospel to the ends of the earth. Christ told His disciples that He would return (John 14:3): "...I go and prepare a place for you, I will come again, and receive you unto myself; that where I am, there ye may be also."

 Write the letter for the correct choice.

3.1 The peace organization that failed was _b._ ✔.
   a. the United Nations   c. the Cold War
   b. the League of Nations

3.2 Practicing tolerance can mean living _b. A_.
   a. at peace   b. at war   c. catastrophically

3.3 Which of these signs will *not* happen before the end time? _a. C_
   a. Many false Christs will appear.
   b. Famines will occur.
   c. A lasting peace will be made.
   d. Many earthquakes will occur.

3.4 The shortest war on record lasted _C._ ✔.
   a. thirty-seven days   b. thirty years   c. less than an hour

 Complete these activities.

3.5 Using the dictionary, explain what diplomacy means and how nations desiring to live in peace use it.
   a. _the conducting of relations between nations_ ✔
   b. _they use it by using their human resources_
      tolerance & understanding the point of view of others.

3.6   Describe the kind of personality that the Antichrist will likely have.

He will most likely have a powerfull and aragant personality (but at first he might have a kind personality to trick the people).

DIVINE JUDGMENT BRINGS PEACE

In the book of Revelation, man and earth are shown during the end of the age. In this book of prophecy, the Saviour of the world, Jesus Christ, is **symbolized** as a conquering lamb. The Christian's enemy, Satan, is shown as having the form of a devouring beast. Two important cities are also in view: Babylon, reminiscent of the spirit of rebellious Babel of old, and new Jerusalem, a beautiful and virtuous city. Babylon is full of sin and is controlled by greedy and ambitious men. In the ensuing conflict the Lamb overcomes His enemies, purges the earth, and establishes His **millennial** reign.

Earth's history climaxes. Just as Noah's generation suffered a universal **catastrophe**, so will those who live during the end time and are aligned with the Antichrist. During that time, an angel will announce that God is ready to pour out **vials** of wrath on the world. This heavenly messenger tells other angels (Revelation 7:3), "Saying, Hurt not the earth, neither the sea, nor the trees, till we have sealed the servants of our God in their foreheads." Thus, the last remnants of God's faithful people on earth will receive assurance that they will not be destroyed along with those who have followed the Antichrist. After the saints will have been sealed, angels will begin emptying vials of God's wrath upon the earth. The topography of the earth will be rearranged; mountains and islands will be moved out of their places. The sun and moon are eclipsed and will be darkened at various intervals. Stars will begin streaking out of the sky toward earth. Some of them fall into the oceans and contaminate part of the water, killing marine life. Rivers will be polluted with bitterness, killing many people.

A **cataclysmic** judgment of fire will also come upon the earth prior to the end of history. The Bible says (II Peter 3:10), ". . .The heavens shall pass away with a great noise, and the elements shall melt with fervent heat, the earth also and the works that are therein shall be burned up." Satan, the beast, and the beast's false prophet will also be judged by fire (Revelation 20:10): "And the devil that deceived them was cast into the lake of fire and brimstone, where the beast and the false prophet are, and shall be tormented day and night forever and ever." In view of the coming judgment, Peter gave Christians this admonition (II Peter 3:11-13): "Seeing then that all these things shall be dissolved, what manner of persons ought ye to be in all holy conversation and godliness. Looking for and hasting unto the coming of the day of God, wherein the heavens being on fire shall be dissolved, and the elements shall melt with fervent heat? Nevertheless we, according to His promise, look for new heavens and a new earth, wherein dwelleth righteousness."

Complete these statements.

3.7   In the book of Revelation, Jesus Christ is symbolized by a conquering
       lamb ✓.

3.8   Besides Babylon, an important city mentioned in Revelation is
       Jerusalem ✓.

3.9   During the end time the topography of the earth will be _rearranged_ ✓

Complete these activities.

Look up the following Scriptures and give your answer from the Scripture text indicated.

3.10   According to Psalm 19:1, what two witnesses continually tell all men that there
       is a living God? a. _the heavens_ ✓ and b. _skies firmament_

3.11   The twenty-seventh book of the Old Testament was written by a prophet who
       told of end-time events. Who was he? _John Daniel_

3.12   According to Romans 2:16, a day is coming when "God shall
       judge ✓ the secrets of men."

3.13   According to Isaiah 9:6 Christ is called the Prince of _Peace_ ✓ .

Millenial reign begins. Christ has the name *King of Kings, and Lord of Lords,* indicative of His might to conquer and His right to rule. According to Revelation 20:6, Christ will reign with His saints on the earth for a thousand years, a millennium. His rule will be established after His enemies are rendered powerless or destroyed.

During the millennium, the earth and its inhabitants will be at peace. Isaiah portrays this time of peace in these words (Isaiah 11:6-9):

> The wolf also shall dwell with the lamb, and the leopard shall lie down with the kid; and the calf and the young lion and the fatling together; and a little child shall lead them. And the cow and the bear shall feed; their young ones shall lie down together; and the lion shall eat straw like the ox. And the sucking child shall play on the hole of the asp, and the weaned child shall put his hand on the cockatrice's den. They shall not hurt nor destroy in all my holy mountain. . . .

Although the millennium will be an ideal time of peace, it will not continue unchanged. Indeed, conditions on the earth will be made better after the millennium ends. John describes the world after the millennium in these words: (Revelation 21:1-5)

> And I saw a new heaven and a new earth: for the first heaven and the first earth were passed away; and there was no more sea. And I John saw the holy city, new Jerusalem, coming down from God out of heaven, prepared as a bride adorned for her husband. And I heard a great voice out of heaven saying, Behold, the tabernacle of God is with men, and he will dwell with them, and they shall be his people, and God himself shall be with them, and be their God. And God shall wipe away all tears from their eyes; and there shall be no more death, neither sorrow, nor crying, neither shall there be any more pain: for the former things are passed away. And he that sat upon the throne said, Behold, I make all things new. . . .

Complete these statements.

3.14 A millennium is a _____1,000_____ ✓ years in time.

3.15 Christ will reign during the millennium with His _____saints_____ ✓ .

3.16 The new Jerusalem will come from ~~God in~~ _____heaven_____ .

Answer these questions.

3.17 During the millennium, what will happen to the diet of carnivorous creatures?
_____the carnivorous creatures will not eat meat_____ ✓
_____

3.18 In the new heaven and new earth what five things will have passed away and be no more?

a. _____tears_____ ✓　　　　d. _____crying_____ ✓

b. _____death_____ ✓　　　　e. _____pain_____ ✓

c. _____sorrow_____ ✓

　　　Before you take this last Self Test, you may want to do one or more of these self checks.

1. _____ Read the objectives. Determine if you can do them.

2. _____ Restudy the material related to any objectives that you cannot do.

3. _____ Use the SQ3R study procedure to review the material:

　　a. **S**can the sections,

　　b. **Q**uestion yourself again (review the questions you wrote initially),

　　c. **R**ead to answer your questions,

　　d. **R**ecite the answers to yourself, and

　　e. **R**eview areas you did not understand.

4. _____ Review all vocabulary, activities, and Self Tests, writing a correct answer for every wrong answer.

SELF TEST 3

Write *true* or *false* (each answer, 1 point).

3.01 _false_ The Sumerians created their civilization during the time of Christ.

3.02 _true_ The Mesopotamians lived along the plains of the Tigris and Euphrates rivers.

3.03 _true_ Gold is malleable and ductile.

3.04 _false_ The great Flood story is a myth.

3.05 _false_ The new Jerusalem is on earth today.

3.06 _false_ The city of Babel and Babylon have always had a good reputation.

3.07 _true_ Airsheds can carry away only a limited amount of smog.

3.08 _true_ Angels will pour vials of wrath upon the earth during the end time.

3.09 _true_ Ur was Abraham's first dwelling place.

3.010 _true_ An alloy is a combination of metals.

Complete these statements (each answer, 3 points).

3.011 The first railroad and turnpike was built in _Rome_ . _England?_

3.012 The first beautiful settlement in the Fertile Crescent was _Babylon_ . _Babel_

3.013 An enormous sheet of ice is called a _glacier_ .

3.014 Two canals that connect large bodies of water are the a. _Panama_ and b. _Suez_ .

3.015 The method of mining introduced by Daniel Jackling is _open pit_ .

3.016 Jesus compared the last days with the days of _Ezekiel_ .

3.017 The last great battle on earth will be the battle of _Armagedon_ .

3.018 The false messiah is known as _the Antichrist_ .

3.019 For every year of peace, man has experienced _seven_ _ten_ years of war.

3.020 The forerunner to the United Nations was the _League of Nations_ .

3.021 The two most common types of fossils fuels are a. _coal_ and b. _petroleum_ .

3.022 Mesopotamia was the "crossroads of the _Middle East_ ."

3.023 Jesus is portrayed as a _Lamb_ _conquering_ in the book of Revelation.

Match these items (each answer, 2 points).

3.024 _b._ Bantu

3.025 _g._ Aztecs

3.026 _c._ Incas

3.027 _f._ Hindus

3.028 _a._ Mayas

3.029 _a._ Phoenicians

3.030 _a._ Chinese

3.031 _f._ Hebrews

3.032 _e._ Minoans

3.033 _c._ Romans

a. Asia
b. Africa
c. South America
d. North America
e. Europe
f. Middle East
g. Mexico
h. Central America

Match these items (each answer, 2 points).

3.034   g.   petrify

3.035   e.   fossil

3.036   d.   fissure

3.037   a.   strata

3.038   c.   inundate

a. layers of rock or soil

b. one who lived before the Flood

c. to flood or submerge under water

d. an opening or crack in the surface of the earth

e. the preserved imprints or remains of animal or plant life in rock

f. Egyptian form of writing

g. to turn soft material into a stony substance

Answer these questions (each answer, 5 points).

3.039   How were fossil fuels formed? _Fossil fuels were formed by when during the flood plants and animals were moved under the ground in areas — and later turned into oil, coal etc. Oil & coal were formed from dead animals & plants under the pressure of tons of rocks & mud over thousands of years._

3.040   How will the earth be changed just before the millennium? _The earth will be rearranged. Mountains will be shifted and etc. Stars will fall into the oceans, killing marine life. Rivers will be poisoned._

3.041   How will life in the new heaven and new earth differ from life today? _carniverous animals will not eat meat, there will be peace and there will be no tears or crying or pain or sorrow or death._

80 / 100

Before taking the LIFEPAC Test, you may want to do one or more of these self checks.

1. _____ Read the objectives. Check to see if you can do them.

2. _____ Restudy the material related to any objectives that you cannot do.

3. _____ Use the SQ3R study procedure to review the material.

4. _____ Review activities, Self Tests, and LIFEPAC vocabulary words.

5. _____ Restudy areas of weakness indicated by the last Self Test.